# Dance Musicality:
# a Biblical and Christian Perspective

EUAL A. PHILLIPS, JR.

Copyright Notice

Dance Musicality: a Biblical and Christian Perspective

© 2020, Eual Abraham Phillips, Jr.

eual.b.blessed@gmail.com

www.eualphillips.com

KDP ISBN: 9798592669293

**Christ Center for Dance and the Arts Mission Statement**

Our mission is to teach and empower people to minister for the Lord through the arts.

# Contents

# Introduction

## Key Concept

All dancers need to develop a biblical and heavenly sense of musicality. Here's why: every music artist, whether they realize it or not, dreams of people dancing to their music. There is not a single music artist who does not think about how their music will impact someone or something; they want their music to influence people's hearts, movements, minds, etc. Artistry means nothing it does not communicate to and inspire those who engage in such work.

For decades songs have also been more popular when there has been a named dance. Whenever there is a named dance associated with the song, the song skyrockets in sales and publicity. Nowadays, we say that the song and dance go viral together. Two examples of this phenomenon include "The Twist," the "Electric Slide," and even the "Tootsie Roll." Other more recent examples at the turn of the millennium are the "Yur," "Watch Me Whip," "Watch Me Nae Nae." These dances have helped to drive a song into the generation that the songs were released in. Based on that principle alone, we can conclude the following phrase as a key concept that will tie together everything that you will learn about dance musicality from a Christian perspective.

Dance is the evidence of being captivated by sound.

Dance musicality is about how dancers hear, interpret, and dance to music. This course combines the Biblical, spiritual, and scientific principles to help dancers develop a deeper understanding of how dance is the evidence of being captivated by a sound. In this course, you will discover and discuss the basic principles of the power at work when you dance and make song selections. Ultimately, you will possess an understanding of how these principles contribute to a lifestyle of worship and enhance your ministry in the worship arts.

Objectives

Here is a list of objectives that will serve as a roadmap to understand the key concept of dance musicality from a Christian perspective.

*Dance is the evidence of being captivated by sound.*

- Define sound and movement using biblical and scientific principles.
- Evaluate the impact of music and dance on atmospheres.

- Define key terminology of dance musicality in order to discuss the significance of discerning the timing or meter of music.
- Define song selection in order to discuss the challenges of selecting songs for worship.
- Define audible and inaudible sounds as they pertain to movement in worship arts.
- Distinguish the difference between the sound of unholy and holy fear in order to discuss the importance of operating and resonating in the holy fear of God.
- Distinguish the difference between spontaneous and prophetic sounds in order to evaluate their appropriate applications in the ministry of worship arts.
- Discuss the challenges of being accepted as a worship artist.

## Biblical vs. Christian Perspective

Some of you may be wondering why the title of this book includes the "biblical" and "Christian" perspectives. The average person may think that they are the same, but they are quite different. A person with a biblical perspective or worldview will approach life and its problems primarily from the word of God. If the word of God does not inspire the solution to a problem, then the solution is of humanistic origin. Within this text, you will consistently find scriptures that support the concept of musicality in worship arts ministry, with emphasis in dance ministry.

On the other hand, the Christian perspective or worldview is often tied to three events, creation, fall, and redemption, with emphasis on the redemptive work of Jesus Christ. The Christian perspective allows an individual to recognize the value of all creation, human and nonhuman, through the lens of Christ. A common philosophy held by Christian educators includes equipping people and maturing them in the application of their gifts for God. Thus, the Christian perspective enables me, the educator, to redeem concepts within dance and worship arts and then urge the reader to use these teachings help them become more mature in their gifting.

## 01 – What is Sound?

According to Merriam-Webster, sound is "defined as the mechanical radiant energy that is transmitted by longitudinal pressure waves in a material medium (such as air) and is the objective cause of hearing." Material medium can also be worded as the "state of matter." Therefore, this definition indicates that sound exerts pressure on any state of matter (solid, liquid, gas, and plasma). Depending on when you went to school, this information may be entirely new to you, but pressure can be exerted on all of these states of matter.

In chemistry and physics, it is understood that on a molecular level, solids are not completely frozen. Solids vibrate in place and are sometimes difficult to separate under normal circumstances. Solids are compressible, moldable, and are strongly attracted to one another like magnets. Liquids rotate around one another but easily separate because they have a lower attraction to each other. Gases prefer separation to the point that they exhibit an elastic motion, by which they collide with one another at incredibly high speeds. Since each state of matter is made up of atoms, we will define **sound** as the mechanical radiant energy that applies pressure on atmospheres. Always keep in mind that sound can travel through any medium, sphere of atoms, or atmosphere. Throughout each teaching, unless otherwise noted, we will most commonly refer to the gaseous state of matter when discussing atmospheres.

*Sound is the mechanical radiant energy that applies pressure on atmospheres.*

To provide more insight on exerting pressure on atmospheres, we will refer to the biblical analogy of the potter and the clay.

> Then the word of the Lord came to me. He said, "Can I not do with you, Israel, as this potter does?" declares the Lord. "Like clay in the hand of the potter, so are you in my hand, Israel. [7] If at any time I announce that a nation or kingdom is to be uprooted, torn down and destroyed, [8] and if that nation I warned repents of its evil, then I will relent and not inflict on it the disaster I had planned. And if at another time I announce that a nation or kingdom is to be built up and planted, [10] and if it does evil in my sight and does not obey me, then I will reconsider the good I had intended to do for it.
>
> "Now therefore say to the people of Judah and those living in Jerusalem, 'This is what the Lord says: Look! I am preparing a disaster for you and

devising a plan against you. So turn from your evil ways, each one of you, and reform your ways and your actions.' But they will reply, 'It's no use. We will continue with our own plans; we will all follow the stubbornness of our evil hearts.'" (NIV, Jeremiah 18:5-12)

The analogy and insight from these verses concerning dance and musicality are as follows: as the potter sculpts the clay, the dancer and musician sculpt the atmosphere. In order to sculpt or shape anything, the individual requires a working material. Potters work with solids or semi-solids, meaning that their working material is clay. For the dancer and the musician, the working material is the air or the atmosphere, which is of the gaseous state of matter. So, the dancer and musician operate with a different state of matter than a potter but share similar operations.

---

*As the potter sculpts the clay, the dancer and musician sculpt the atmosphere.*

---

Air becomes breath when it carries a fragrance. Air can be captivated by our worship. All of creation can be captivated by worship and is commanded to praise the Lord (Psalm 148,150). As a dancer or worship artist, your movement in worship is the fragrance that causes the air to become the breath that praises the Lord. This is the scientific reasoning and explanation as to why everything that has breath praises the Lord. All of creation has been given a capacity to worship. He designed everything to be captivated by who He is, including us. Therefore dance, or any type of movement done as an act of worship, is important when ministry is married to music or song.

*As a dancer or worship artist, your movement in worship is the fragrance that causes the air to become the breath that praises the Lord.*

At the end of the day, whether you are a musician, dancer, or a psalmist, your worship exerts pressure on atmospheres. Even if you work a job as a bread baker, the atmosphere responds to the work of a baker by carrying the fragrance of breads and pastries that the baker makes. Every type of work that involves movement releases a fragrance into the atmosphere and attempts to grab the attention of creation and bring it into some type of captivity or captivation.

## 02 – Discerning the Time to Dance

<u>The Significance of Time</u>

> There is a time for everything and a
> season for every activity under the
> heavens:
>
> a time to be born and a time to die,
> a time to plant and a time to uproot,
> a time to kill and a time to heal,
> a time to tear down and a time to build,
> a time to weep and a time to laugh,
> a time to mourn and a time to dance,
> a time to scatter stones and a time to
> gather them,
> a time to embrace and a time to refrain
> from embracing,
> a time to search and a time to give up,
> a time to keep and a time to throw
> away,
> a time to tear and a time to mend,
> a time to be silent and a time to speak,
> a time to love and a time to hate,
> a time for war and a time for peace.
>
> What do workers gain from their toil?
> I have seen the burden God has laid on
> the human race. He has made
> everything beautiful in its time. He
> has also set eternity in the human
> heart; yet no one can fathom what
> God has done from beginning to end. I

know that there is nothing better for people than to be happy and to do good while they live. That each of them may eat and drink, and find satisfaction in all their toil—this is the gift of God. I know that everything God does will endure forever; nothing can be added to it and nothing taken from it. God does it so that people will fear him. (NIV, Ecclesiastes 3:1-14)

Developing a sensitivity to the timings of music is so important. Why? Because there is a timing to everything. When you are provided with a song, a rhythm, and a sequence of notes, it is up to use as the dancer to decide what you will do within the allotted time that has been provided. What work will you accomplish within the timing of the music? What burden will God lay upon you as you dance? What will you make beautiful with the time that you have in the song? What is it about eternity that God wants you to portray in the dance? What are you going to do with the time He has given you within the space of a song so that people will be captivated in His holy fear?

This is why you must develop a sensitivity to music. By becoming educated, skilled, and versed in dancing musicality, you are essentially preparing yourself to maximize the time and space that God has provided for you to dance in. Let's begin learning the time terminology of dance musicality.

<u>An Overview of Basic Dance Musicality Terms</u>

A **beat** is defined as "a division or unit of musical time in a measure" (Kuhn, 1999, 99). The most common number of beats in a measure of music is four. The beat is the primary reference from which the dancer decides how to dance, whether it is to the beat, against the beat, depending on the choreography (Grant, 2017). The **meter** is defined as "the pattern in which a steady succession of rhythmic pulses is organized ... one complete pattern or its equivalent in length is termed a measure or bar" (Randel 1986, 489). At the composer's discretion, music can be written with multiple beats per measure. The most common meter is known as "4/4 time," which means that there are four beats per measure and that the quarter note is the dominant beat. When performing a dance in the style of a waltz, it is typically performed to a meter of "3/4" time, which means that there are three beats per measure while still relying on the quarter note to be the dominant beat. Other less common meters can include "5/4" (5 beats per measure defined by a quarter note) and "7/8" (7 beats per measure defined by eight notes. The meter of a song often serves to support dance movement and provide the template that gives a song its unique characteristics.

**Tempo** is defined as "the specific speed at which music is performed" (Latham 2002). Tempo is measured in beats per minute (bpm). Learning to dance at varying tempos often heightens the dancer's listening skills and muscle control. Throughout the process, the dancer learns to pay attention to and select for the quality of their movement, depending on their level of skill (Grant, 2017).

The **accent** is defined as "In measured music, the first beat of each measure is the strong beat and thus carries a metrical accent" (Randel ,1986, 3). The purpose of the accent is to keep the dancer alert (Grant, 2017). If as a musician, when sight-reading music for the first time ever gets lost, they are to look at the conductor or listen for the rhythm of the music to find the accent, or the first beat, in order to try and pick up where they left off.

**Duration** is defined as "The time that a sound or silence lasts" —Randel (1986, 247). Most often, dancers try to learn choreography in steps by taking well-defined movements and grouping them together. However, when musicality is involved, it is better to match choreography with the duration of musical phrases (Grant, 2017). This causes the steps to feel less isolated and more like one continuous skill or long movement that sometimes appears to have no distinct beginning or end to those viewing the performance.

**Articulation** is defined as "The way notes are joined to one another when forming a musical line, e.g. staccato, legato, tenuto, glissando, slur, phrase mark, accents, sforzandos, rinforzandos, etc. — Dolmetsch Online Music Dictionary (2015a). Articulation is about embedding ordinary music with expression, which also adds to the distinct qualities of musical composition (Grant, 2017).

**Rhythmic variation** is defined as "At its simplest, rhythm may be thought of as the disposition of strong (or accented) and weak (or unaccented) beats in a piece of music. —Dolmetsch Online Music Dictionary (2015c)". It can also be referred to as syncopation, where accents are added to sub-beats and off-beats. Rhythmic variation makes room for two or more choreographed rhythms to exist at the same time within a musical phrase (Grant, 2017). Rhythmic variation can also be used to make choreography more complex because it can cause the dancer to change the duration of their movements between accented and unaccented beats.

Finally, a **canon** is defined as "A musical form in which a (second, third, fourth, etc.) line starting later than the one before it matches it note for note but such that the parts overlap. —Dolmetsch Online Music Dictionary (2015b). In simple terms, a canon is similar to performing a round, like singing the song "Row, Row, Row Your Boat." Just as one person will begin a musical phrase, another person can start the same musical phrase at a later time, thus creating countermelodies, or counterpoint in the context of dance. Just as countermelodies make a listening experience richer, a canon will enrich the visual experience and causes dancers to develop aural, proprioceptive, and spatial awareness (Grant, 2017).

<u>Be Sober and Sensitive</u>

> Be very careful, then, how you live— not as unwise but as wise, making the most of every opportunity, because the days are evil. Therefore, do not be foolish, but understand what the Lord's will is. Do not get drunk on wine, which leads to debauchery. Instead, be filled with the Spirit, speaking to one another with psalms, hymns, and songs from the Spirit. Sing and make music from your heart to the Lord, always giving thanks to God the Father for everything, in the name of our Lord Jesus Christ. (NIV, Ephesians 5:15-20)

After going through these dance musicality terms, I challenge you to no longer be unwise but to be rich in wisdom concerning every movement you make in your dance. Do not allow your dance to be a sloppy byproduct of being insensitive to the musical timings that God has created for you to participate in. Be filled with the Spirit, and stay sensitive to the psalms, hymns, and songs from the Spirit. When God signals a song to be sung from heaven, it is because

He desires to bring people into a higher life of sobriety. He is trying to captivate people with a song. Therefore, I encourage you to take up the responsibility of being a visual expression of the music that He provides from the high life of heaven. Discern the times within the music and dance!

## 03 – The Impact of Song Selection

<u>Defining Song Selection</u>

In worship arts, song selection can be defined as the selective pressure applied to the physical and spiritual atmosphere. Remember, it was previously mentioned that the potter uses a pottery wheel as a dancer uses a song. We have this solid state of matter that can be molded, reshaped, or reformed, but it's on a spinning wheel. Placing the clay on the spinning wheel actually gives the potter more control over forming the clay. The song does the same thing. The song applies pressure to the atmosphere, causing the air molecules to spin. The air molecules will begin to align to the frequencies that are being emitted by the song playing from your chosen sound system. Therefore, these tools prepare the working material for obedience to your movements.

When the potter puts the clay on the pottery wheel and causes it to spin, it becomes easier to manipulate the clay, or in other words, the clay becomes more susceptible to the potter's movements. The clay has to obey according to the hand or the pressure applied by the potter's hands. This is what happens with songs. You begin to participate in shifting the atmosphere in such a way that the air becomes more obedient or sensitive to your movements because it is looking to carry the fragrance of worship. Air becomes breath when it carries a fragrance. When you move worshipfully, the air becomes a carrier of the fragrance released by your worship, thus, becoming breath. Therefore, the song is important when attempting to be a vessel that shifts the atmosphere.

## Types of Pressure in the Bible

There are two types of pressure that can be exerted in atmospheres and on other objects. The first is the weight of sin.

> Therefore we also, since we are surrounded by so great a cloud of witnesses, let us lay aside every weight, and the sin which so easily ensnares *us,* and let us run with endurance the race that is set before us. (NKJV, Hebrews 12:1)

Notice that sin is a weight that can be set aside. Sin has the ability to hinder our movements. It prevents individuals from developing the endurance necessary to appropriately apply their faith toward God.

Within the same scripture, the writer gives us a good reason why we need to cast off the weights of sin. Previously, I mentioned that the atmosphere will respond to your movements and carry the breath of worship generated from your movements. The writer mentions the cloud of witnesses. We should want to cast off the weight of sin because of the cloud. We have to develop a consciousness of the fact that we have an audience in heaven that is watching and cheering us on in our race. We need **cloud consciousness** if we want to worship God without the weight of sin.

The second pressure is the weight of God's glory.

> For our light affliction, which is but for a moment, is working for us a far more exceeding *and* eternal weight of glory, while we do not look at the things which are seen, but at the things which are not seen. For the things which are seen *are* temporary, but the things which are not seen *are* eternal. (NKJV, 2 Corinthians 4:17-18)

Even God's glory has a weight to it, and it can actually activate or suspend our movements, depending on what God wants to do with His glory. We need momentary light afflictions in our lives in order to prepare us for the movements that God wants us to perform in our worship. This weight of glory is not meant to oppress and hold us back but rather trains and disciplines us to have supernatural endurance, which is what the weight of sin tries to prevent us from attaining.

Keeping these two types of weight in mind, here are two questions for you.

1. What type of sound captivates you? (Instrumental music is no exception!)
2. What type of pressure do you want to exert on the atmosphere as you worship?

The Challenges of Song Selection

I highly advise that you question where songs come from. If they are not coming from the right place, then people will be captivated by the wrong spirit. Let's review a song that can be used as an example of the importance of song selection because people can have varying opinions and arguments about the interpretation of this song's lyrics.

> Before I spoke a word, You were
> singing over me.
> You have been so, so good to me.
> Before I took a breath, You breathed
> Your life in me.
> You have been so, so kind to me
> Oh, the overwhelming, never-ending,
> reckless love of God! (Asbury,
> Reckless Love, 2018)

Did you notice anything that could be wrong with the song? The potential problem with the song is the use of the word "reckless" to describe God's love. Do not miss the intent behind what is being said. This is not an attempt to slander Cory Asbury, the writer, or question his walk with God. I am 100% positive that

Cory Asbury meant well when he used the word "reckless" to describe God's love. My intent in all of this is not to condemn you if you differ in opinion, but rather that you would become soberer in your thoughts concerning who God is.

If we educate ourselves, we will realize that reckless means "marked by lack of caution; irresponsible" (Merriam-Webster). This is not an accurate description of God's character. Let's refer to the scriptures to get a more accurate glimpse of God's love.

> For he chose us in him before the creation of the world to be holy and blameless in his sight. In love, he predestined us for adoption to sonship through Jesus Christ, in accordance with his pleasure and will... (NIV, Ephesians 1:4-5, 2011).

According to Ephesians, God's love is not reckless. He is planned for us all to be here in all of His wisdom. This is the type of love in which an individual makes plans to spend the rest of their life with them, similarly to a marriage covenant. Reckless love has no clear plan for the future and direction for the people that are involved in this pseudo-covenant. This type of love resembles the love that we may have tried to imitate when we did not know God. Even though God loves the world, He does not love the world with the world's definition of love. Reckless love implies irresponsibility and lack of caution for the other individual involved. Reckless love permits someone to freely leave the relationship when the person selfishly does not get what they expect from the relationship or if there is a strong offense between the two.

God's love is a hardcore truth that ought not be perverted. If any word could be used to replace reckless, the next best fit would probably be radical, but I am sure radical just does not fit the meter of the song as well as reckless does. Anyway, this is why we must be careful of the songs that are chosen for worship, even if the person is a reputable Christian. We must check them ourselves. When we worship, we must make sure that all the music we use is consistent with the heart of God, the word of God, and the knowledge of God.

## Taking Songs into Captivity

In order to check our songs, we must take songs into captivity first. Music not only can be used as a weapon to destroy strongholds, but it can lay down foundations for new ones. Not every stronghold is bad. If we are the temple of the Holy Spirit, then that means we ourselves are being built as a stronghold. We must study our songs. We must be yoked to the song. The song must have us in captivity and we must have the song in captivity. This is a symbiotic relationship similar to how God wants us to be in supernatural unity (John 17:20-24).

For the weapons of our warfare are not carnal but mighty in God for pulling down strongholds, casting down arguments and every high thing that exalts itself against the knowledge of God, bringing every thought into captivity to the obedience of Christ... (NKJV, 2 Corinthians 10:4-5)

We are supposed to take every thought and imagination and present it to Christ, including songs. If you practice this, this will make you into a more sensitive worshipper. By simply practicing the discipline of taking a song to Him and allowing Him to decide whether the song selection is worthy enough to represent Him, you will be more readily used by God in shifting the atmosphere and bringing the atmosphere into obedience. In other words, before we can bring an atmosphere into obedience, we must present to Him the tools, the songs, the equipment, the choreography, and ourselves for obedience to Christ. Attempting to shift atmospheres without obedience and submission to Christ has several consequences on the ego that will not be explored at this moment.

Maintaining the Standards of Song Selection

In 2019, I attended a worship conference and asked one of the session leaders their opinion on music or songs that have erroneous language, such as "Reckless Love." I asked that question because I was taught that songs can disciple generations of people, which is true; we are still being discipled by David's psalms to this day and are composing countless arrangements using scriptures across the entire bible. As a teacher, I wanted to ask that hard question about "Reckless Love" because I was truly convicted.

This worship leader replied by saying that English is a primary example of a langue that is always changing the meaning of words. He even said that 20 years from now, Merriam-Webster could even add a definition of reckless that includes being an exuberant lover of God. Oftentimes, in other languages, the meaning of words often does not change when translated.

One of the things I do not like to do with people is debate with them over their beliefs. I prefer to hear their beliefs, go to God, and then allow God to reveal the truth to me. This is what Paul writes in 2 Corinthians 10:4-5. Jesus also recommends this in John 7:16-18. So to avoid debate, I accepted what I believed to be his opinion at the time, thanked him for his response, and sat down.

After spending time with God, I developed the defense against such an argument presented by the worship leader. If we can change the meaning of any word, then that means the words of men are fallible. The word of God is infallible and does not change. This implies that the words of men are subject to lies, deceit, and corruption, whereas God's word is incorruptible truth. God's identity cannot be wrapped up in lies or misconceptions of who He is because our concept of Him often affects our faith in Him. If we can simply change the meaning of things instead of exploring the deep truths and their existing definitions, then this can ultimately lead to licentiousness. This type of mentality can even encourage believers to misinterpret scriptures because they might have changed the meaning of the word of God to make it relevant to their personal context or imagination, rather than interpreting God's word based on the context it was originally in and then comparing it to other instances in the bible. We have often associated licentiousness with sexual immorality and other obvious sins, but we neglect the idea that licentiousness can occur with the application and misuse of God's word being wrapped up in our own vain imaginations.

Let's examine an additional argument that was brought up at the worship conference that I attended. If you consider a new convert, the new convert might say that God's love is reckless because God risked everything to save him or her. The argument continued on the premise that reckless could be used as slang, similar to how people use wicked cool, mad stupid, or stupid cool. No matter what generation you are born into, slang vocabulary is often commonly used by teenagers and young adults. If the individual matures beyond the young adult stage, they will not find themselves using slang anymore to describe life. They will describe life accurately and for what it truly is. Even for someone who is educated like me, I would hope that the word reckless, as a slang, would simply phase out of my vocabulary. As a more mature person, I now begin to associate reckless behavior to the past, such as making poor and selfish decisions in life, such as having too much wine to drink. Reckless is also typically associated with negative behavior. Yes, there are negative consequences that the Father outlines throughout the bible, but the Father does not exhibit negative behaviors. Otherwise, He would lose His right to be called Father.

After having a conversation with the Father, here is what He said to me from the perspective of being a teacher.

> So Christ himself gave the apostles, the prophets, the evangelists, the pastors and teachers, to equip his people for works of service so that the body of Christ may be built up until we all reach unity in the faith and in the knowledge of the Son of God and become mature, attaining to the whole measure of the fullness of Christ.
>
> Then we will no longer be infants, tossed back and forth by the waves, and blown here and there by every wind of teaching and by the

cunning and craftiness of people in their deceitful scheming. Instead, speaking the truth in love, we will grow to become in every respect the mature body of him who is the head, that is, Christ. From him the whole body, joined and held together by every supporting ligament, grows and builds itself up in love, as each part does its work. (NIV, Ephesians 4:11-16)

Since every believer has to start someplace in their faith, it is acceptable for someone who is new and immature to have a perspective of God's love as being reckless. God is incredibly merciful and patient with us regarding how we have perceived Him in error in our relationship with Him. However, every believer is called to a mature and correct perspective of God at some point in time. The long-term goal of maturity cannot be lowered or negated, but at the same time, it's okay to lower the barrier to entry based on the believer's state of mind.

One of the reasons why the body of Christ has not reached maturity is because we hold on to antiquated and immature mindsets of who God is. There is a tendency for members of the body to think of God the same way they did when they first got saved; they may have been saved for ten or twenty years and have not made significant advancements in knowledge of our Lord and Savior, Jesus. Our revelation and love for Jesus should be getting deeper, longer, wider, and higher than it has ever been in the past. Our perception of God becomes simplified and complex at the same time, but ultimately, it becomes fully developed.

As a teacher, my greatest desire is for my students to reach full maturity. If a believer's best descriptor of God's love is still rooted in the word "reckless" after being saved for 10-20 years, then they have not progressed toward the whole measure of the fullness of Christ. For someone like myself, who is a seasoned believer, using the word reckless is a regression of my revelatory knowledge of God. It is the equivalent of how the Jewish people studied the law of Moses, the Ten Commandments for centuries, but when Jesus said, "Love your neighbor," the people responded by saying, "Who is my neighbor?" Their revelation of God had become completely stagnant because they never realized that the law of Moses was pointing to God's love. Their antiquated mindsets prevented them from receiving Jesus. Likewise, we should not allow antiquated thoughts become strongholds that prevent us from receiving the fullness of God.

Therefore, song selection is important. The song you choose could be communicating something that you do not want to communicate. The song could be setting up an atmosphere that caters to immature believers but does not advance the knowledge of Jesus in such a way that produces maturity within the body of Christ. Who is your audience? Who will witness your ministry to God? This is what you must think about because your ministry will apply pressure not just on the atmosphere but also on people's spirits and souls.

## 04 – Impact of Movement on Sound

Welcome back; this is your instructor, you'll be blessed making it clear and making it plain; may my teaching fall upon you like a Refreshing Spring rain all right in the lesson you are about to embark on is called the impact of movement is on sale if you have not done, watch the videos on lessons one and two what is found in the impact of songs like you make sure you cover that material so that everything makes sense all right so you're almost done with module 1 the sound of dance get excited because you are about to be a very powerful dancer, let's begin; so first of all

<u>Inaudible Sound</u>

Sound does not have to be heard by your ear in order to have an impact. Every creature is designed to hear certain frequencies of sound. Human hearing is limited to certain frequencies. Thus, there are two types of frequencies that are outside of our hearing range: infrasound and ultrasound.

Let me define these inaudible sounds to humans. Keep in mind that our perception of sound is relative to human hearing. Infrasound has a low-frequency and a long-wavelength. Therefore, these sounds can travel longer distances. Elephants have more than one type of communication. We tend to be more familiar with their high-pitched roar, but they can communicate through vibrations in the earth. These vibrations can travel for miles.

Ultrasound has a high frequency but a short wavelength. Ultrasound travels a shorter distance than infrasound. It is more easily disrupted too. Consider a pregnant woman receiving her ultrasound. Why do they apply gel to the surface of the body before using ultrasound? Well, each type of atmosphere or medium can carry sound. Each medium has a different capacity. Ultrasound does not travel well through the air. Rather, it travels quite well in liquids. The frequency of ultrasound is so high that the air disrupts its ability to travel. Thus, if no gel is used, much of the signal from the ultrasound is lost because of the air that will try to move between the skin and the ultrasound device. The gel ensures that the signal is not lost so that it can reach the inner parts of the body and produce an image. At the end of the day, even though the human ear cannot hear these sounds, they exist, and there is scientific evidence of their existence.

One practical example I will provide for you concerning the impact of movement on sound is the cricket. I have lived in an apartment that is frequently visited by crickets in the transition from summer to the fall season in the United States. If you were to try to casually approach a cricket, it would likely jump away before you truly get near to it. If you approach a cricket very slowly, then you increase your likelihood of getting closer before it becomes startled and moves. How are crickets able to do this? Crickets have hairs that detect the movement of air molecules. When we approach them, they get quiet so that they can try to hear our movements over their own chirping. Therefore, crickets can hear our movements even though we cannot.

So, because I know that crickets respond to the sound of my movements, I came up with my own method in my attempts to catch them. I would use the vacuum cleaner. The vacuum cleaner is so loud that it can mask the sound of my movements. Using the vacuum cleaner does not guarantee that I will catch it, but it significantly increases the likelihood that the cricket will get sucked up. The rest of the skill in capturing these crickets is hand-eye coordination because eventually, they will be able to sense the movement of the vacuum hose.

Overall, if the crickets can hear our movements and respond to them, then how much more can the heavenly hosts and demons hear and respond to our movements when we operate in our authority in Christ! Our movements have influence. When an officer raises his badge, he does it from the place of authority. It becomes a signal for you to consider submission to the officer. If we do not submit to the atmosphere that the police officer is trying to create, then there will likely be negative consequences. The same could be said about spiritual matters. There are things that happen in the spirit in our worship, whether it be song or dance. If there are things in the spirit that do not respond to our movements, then that means there may actually be some negative consequences, or you may not have reached a level of authority where your dance or worship brings things into submission. However, these are not the only reasons why an atmosphere may not shift. At the end of all of this, there is a difference between having faith to shift atmospheres and having the authority to facilitate atmospheric shifts.

Audible Sound

Now that we have explored the inaudible sounds, let us return to the human range of hearing. Movement can also create audible sounds. The lion tamer at the circus uses a whip to instruct animals. It is a powerful movement that often commands authority and produces intimidation. If you have ever been disciplined by your parents with a physical object, you can hear the whip of the instrument of choice before it even strikes your body. It is a sound that reminds a person of discipline and being prepared to receive instruction.

The buzzing of insects comes from the flapping of their wings. Insect wings move at such a high frequency that we cannot hear them when they are far away, but when they are close to our ears, we are in detection range of the sound of their wings.

When playing a musical instrument, such as the recorder, the movement and placement of our fingers affect the passage of air. Changing the movement and direction of the air affects the speed at which the air escapes the instrument, which is what determines the frequency of the music note. Even on a windy day, as the air passes through branches, the air extracts the praises of the trees, allowing you to hear the rustling leaves and the gentle swaying of the branches. At the end of the day, all movement creates sound, no matter how grand or minute the movement is. So, dancers and other worship artists who desire to be masters of their movement: You have influence over all creation and people. You can even extend this influence into the heavenly realms.

## 05 – Being a Sound Receiver

We are all designed like tuning forks; we resonate and respond to sounds and pressures that are exerted on us. When a baby cries, it exerts pressure on the parents to act on his or her needs. Surveys say that a baby's cry is one of the most annoying sounds that can be generated in the world. Although this sound can be incredibly annoying, the child is given an inherent power to release a sound that captivates the parents and provokes them into action. Scratching a chalkboard the wrong way produces a sound that literally sends a chill down the spine of anyone in the vicinity. I'm sure that if you have ever been in a technologically deprived classroom, then you are familiar with this sound. This action provokes a response from our bodies. All these different sounds signal the execution of particle movement down to the atomic level.

<u>The Sound of Unholy Fear</u>

> A champion named Goliath, who was from Gath, came out of the Philistine camp. His height was six cubits and a span. He had a bronze helmet on his head and wore a coat of scale armor of bronze weighing five thousand shekels[b]; on his legs, he wore bronze greaves, and a bronze javelin was slung on his back. His spear shaft was like a weaver's rod, and its iron point

weighed six hundred shekels. His shield bearer went ahead of him.

Goliath stood and shouted to the ranks of Israel, "Why do you come out and line up for battle? Am I not a Philistine, and are you not the servants of Saul? Choose a man and have him come down to me. If he is able to fight and kill me, we will become your subjects; but if I overcome him and kill him, you will become our subjects and serve us." Then the Philistine said, "This day I defy the armies of Israel! Give me a man and let us fight each other." On hearing the Philistine's words, Saul and all the Israelites were dismayed and terrified. (1 Samuel 17:411)

Let's examine the pressure that Goliath exerted on Israel through sound. He exerted fear or a trembling paralysis over the warriors of the nation. In the spirit, Goliath's words become a repetitious and poisonous song in our hearts. We become filled with condemnation and fear. This example shows that sound has both physical and spiritual impacts on our movements. Therefore, it is important to take heed to what you hear and how you hear because it can impact your ability to move with the Holy Spirit when you engage in your art form of worship.

If we examine the sequence of events that occurred, we will notice that Israel saw Goliath first. Then Goliath speaks a message that Israel hears. It is not the sight of Goliath that produces fear; it is not until Israel hears Goliath's message. In the flesh, vision is a prerequisite that influences your perception of sound. As a result, your internal tuning fork will resonate with an unholy fear. The army became captivated by the sound of Goliath. As worship artists, many of us already know that there is a warfare component to our worship. We cannot be captivated by the sound of fear because it will paralyze our true and proper worship to God.

The Sound of Holy Fear

> On the Lord's Day, I was in the Spirit, and I heard behind me a loud voice like a trumpet, which said: "Write on a scroll what you see and send it to the seven churches: to Ephesus, Smyrna, Pergamum, Thyatira, Sardis, Philadelphia and Laodicea."

> I turned around to see the voice that was speaking to me. And when I turned, I saw seven golden lampstands, and among the lampstands was someone like a son of man, dressed in a robe reaching down to his feet and with a golden sash around his chest. The hair on his head was white like

wool, as white as snow, and his eyes were like blazing fire. His feet were like bronze glowing in a furnace, and his voice was like the sound of rushing waters. In his right hand he held seven stars, and coming out of his mouth was a sharp, double-edged sword. His face was like the sun shining in all its brilliance.

When I saw him, I fell at his feet as though dead. Then he placed his right hand on me and said: "Do not be afraid. I am the First and the Last. I am the Living One; I was dead, and now look, I am alive forever and ever! And I hold the keys of death and Hades.

"Write, therefore, what you have seen, what is now and what will take place later. The mystery of the seven stars that you saw in my right hand and of the seven golden lampstands is this: The seven stars are the angels of the seven churches, and the seven lampstands are the seven churches. (NIV, Revelation 1:10-17 NIV)

If we examine the sequence of events that occurred between Jesus and John, we will find a bit of contrast between them. First, Jesus speaks, and then John hears. John then turns to see the voice and then he breaks out into a holy fear. Unlike the scene with

Israel and Goliath, the Lord uses sound to direct our gaze. The critical thing to pay attention to is the source of the sound. In this case, it was the Lord Jesus in his heavenly glory. Therefore, a sound from heaven exerts a pressure that induces holy fear. However, when we are captivated by the fear of the Lord, then this fear prepares us to be messengers of the mysteries of God, which is evidenced by Jesus telling John to prepare to write the book of Revelation.

## The Power of Resonating in Holy Fear

While dance produces a sound that is inaudible to the human ear, vision is still important. When referring to Israel and Goliath, the sound affirmed the vision. When referring to Jesus and John, the vision affirms what was heard. Even though both events have different outcomes, the two events affirm one essential truth: when vision and sound come into agreement, they command a powerful response from those who witness it. Let's return to the encounter with Goliath to examine what happens when a person who has been resonating in the holy fear of the Lord steps onto the battlefield.

> When Eliab, David's oldest brother, heard him speaking with the men, he burned with anger at him and asked, "Why have you come down here? And with whom did you leave those few sheep in the wilderness? I know how conceited you are and how wicked

41

your heart is; you came down only to watch the battle."

"Now, what have I done?" said David. "Can't I even speak?" He then turned away to someone else and brought up the same matter, and the men answered him as before. What David said was overheard and reported to Saul, and Saul sent for him. (NIV, 1 Samuel 17:28-31)

Notice what happens when David steps onto the scene. It is evident that the people on the battlefield were consumed by fear and did not want David to speak. Additionally, the voice of fear tried to send David back to where he came from as if David was an irresponsible worker who would risk his responsibilities for glory. However, even though they tried to silence David's sound, a word still got out to Saul about David's rebuke against the Philistine. Let's examine the words of the man who spent time with God in the wilderness.

But David said to Saul, "Your servant has been keeping his father's sheep. When a lion or a bear came and carried off a sheep from the flock, I went after it, struck it and rescued the sheep from its mouth. When it turned on me, I seized it by its hair, struck it and killed it. Your servant has killed both the lion and the bear; this uncircumcised

Philistine will be like one of them because he has defied the armies of the living God. The Lord who rescued me from the paw of the lion and the paw of the bear will rescue me from the hand of this Philistine." (NIV, 1 Samuel 17:34-37)

Notice the language that David uses in describing the history of victories against animals in the field. David begins sharing his testimony in the first and third person, using words such as "I" and "your servant." Even after David said that he, himself, was the one who killed both the lion and the bear, he closes his testimony by saying that the Lord rescued him. You could almost accuse David of being boastful and maybe even double-minded for switching the conversation like that. However, this is how a man of God, who has spent time worshipping and growing in the holy fear of the Lord, actually speaks. He speaks as if he is one with the Father, similarly to how Jesus often speaks in the gospels. Let's keep reading and analyzing what happened to David before his victory over Goliath.

Then Saul dressed David in his own tunic. He put a coat of armor on him and a bronze helmet on his head. David fastened on his sword over the tunic and tried walking around because he was not used to them.

"I cannot go in these," he said to Saul, "because I am not used to them." So he took them off. Then he took his staff in his hand, chose five smooth stones from the stream, put them in the pouch of his shepherd's bag and, with his sling in his hand, approached the Philistine. (NIV 1 Samuel 17:38-40)

Saul's attempt to dress David in his armor is quite significant. If David had secured a victory in Saul's armor, people probably would have thought that it was Saul who killed Goliath and not David. These pieces of armor physically weighed David down. However, on the spiritual side, the armor applied more pressure on him to suppress the sound that was in him. Even from a physics perspective, when a soldier wears a helmet over his head, usually the helmet covers a significant amount of the face to even change the sound of the person's voice. This helmet literally could have changed the sound of David's message even if he could have made it to the battlefield with the equipment. Anyway, both Saul and the armor had been sitting under the sound of unholy fear. For David to wear the armor, he would be clothing himself in unholy fear. This armor would have hindered the execution of God's judgment against the Philistines. Thankfully, the holy fear of God did not allow David to wear this unholy armor.

Now pay attention to what David did next. Armed with a staff and a sling, David went to a stream and chose five smooth stones and put them in his shepherd's bag. I would even go as far as to argue that the five smooth stones had been sitting under the sound of rushing waters, which could be associated with the sound of the Lord's voice in heaven (Ezekiel 43:2; Revelation 14:2). If this comparison of the stream to the Lord's voice is valid, then that means these stones were already captivated by Jesus and submitted to Him. These actions are significant because David brings tools that had already been consecrated or submitted to God. He approached the battlefield with tools that resonate with the same sound that he developed in the fields with the animals. Now let's proceed to analyze David's message before he experiences victory over Goliath.

> David said to the Philistine, "You come against me with sword and spear and javelin, but I come against you in the name of the Lord Almighty, the God of the armies of Israel, whom you have defied. This day the Lord will deliver you into my hands, and I'll strike you down and cut off your head. This very day I will give the carcasses of the Philistine army to the birds and the wild animals, and the whole world will know that there is a God in Israel. All those gathered here will know that it is not by sword or spear that the Lord saves; for the battle is the Lord's, and he will give all

of you into our hands." (NIV, 1 Samuel 17:45-47)

I hope you realize that David went through several events in a very short period. The goal of these events was to contaminate the sound that David had developed so that the atmosphere would not submit to God. David declared that Goliath came with weapons, but he came to the battlefield in the name of the Lord Almighty and with an anointed message. David came with a sound that not only set Israel free, but it set all of creation free. David was not just speaking to Goliath; he was speaking to every created thing. He was even informing the animals, who were probably being terrorized by the Philistines, that they too would reap a reward by feeding on the carcasses of the Philistines. David was releasing a sound that recaptured the attention of creation and turned it against the Philistines. Creation had been held captive by the Philistines for so long that it was moaning and groaning for the manifestation of a son of God (Romans 8:21-22). This son happened to be David that day.

After learning of David's experience with Goliath from a completely different perspective, I hope you are beginning to understand and value the concept of the sound of your worship. Let me remind you that worship does not always have to involve music, but all worship generates a sound that captivates creation. Creation will recognize this sound and try to join in worship with you. David may have been singing in the fields as he shepherded over the animals, but his shepherding is considered worship as well. When you do anything with gratitude unto the Lord, it is worship that carries the sound of heaven, and it is the sound of the Chief Shepherd, who is Jesus, that accompanied him onto the battlefield against the Philistines. Overall, everything about you needs to be captivated by God, but also a revelation of the Lord Jesus. Therefore, I leave you with this final statement: the degree to which you are captivated by God will also be the degree to which the atmospheres will be captivated and shifted by you.

## 06 – Intelligible vs. Unintelligible Sound

Now, brothers and sisters, if I come to you and speak in tongues, what good will I be to you, unless I bring you some revelation or knowledge or prophecy or word of instruction? (NIV, 1 Corinthians 14:6)

Let us begin to dive into the concept of intelligible sound. Like speaking in tongues, anything that produces a sound must carry with it some type of meaning or message; otherwise, the utterance is completely useless to humanity. The sound ought to come packaged with revelation, knowledge, prophecy, or a word of instruction.

Again, if the trumpet does not sound a clear call, who will get ready for battle? ⁹ So it is with you. Unless you speak intelligible words with your tongue, how will anyone know what you are saying? You will just be speaking into the air. (NIV, 1 Corinthians 14:8-9)

What Paul was ultimately saying is that the intelligibility of sound affects movement execution. If the trumpet sound is not clear, then the execution is hindered. There are confusion and people cannot go to battle or into war properly. Imagine if the sound of a fire alarm was replaced with the sound of a chirping bird. No one would think to exit the building to escape the fire until they either smelled smoke or the fire reached the room where the people are. By then, you could almost say that it is too late to safely escape in a calm and orderly fashion. Whenever there is a sound that is not properly assigned or clearly communicated, there is room for confusion. It hinders our physical movements just as Goliath's sound paralyzed Israel. On the other hand, when Jesus speaks, He is really trying to stir up a movement in you. Therefore, we can define intelligible sound as the mechanical radiant energy that applies pressure on an atmosphere and motivates its listeners into decisively organized action.

When I was in the marching band in high school and college, the most important thing to do first is to learn the music before going out to the football field to layout drill and choreography. By intimately knowing the music first, I became more confident in carrying out my instructions on the football field. Combining the music with my movements helped me discern where I needed to be positioned on the football field. Pretty soon, the number and size of the steps I needed to take would be embedded into the music that I learned.

To this day, I can still visualize where I was on the football field when I recall the music that was played. Likewise, when we are frequently immersed in the sounds of heaven, we are more likely to execute movements with greater accuracy and precision. At the end of the day, it is vitally important that we make consistent efforts to clearly hear the sounds of heaven because these sounds provide us with revelation, knowledge, prophecy, and words of instructions, which can ultimately be embedded in our movement execution.

## 07 – Spontaneous vs. Prophetic Sound

As we go through the differences between spontaneous and prophetic sound, it is important that you remember that when we speak of sound, we are referring to song, music, mime, and any movement that influences atmospheres. Some of you hearing this the first time are probably thinking that spontaneous and prophetic sound are the same and probably use them interchangeably. However, they are not the same. Here, I define five principles that distinguish spontaneous sound from prophetic sound.

**Principle 1:** **Spontaneous sound** edifies self; **prophetic sound** edifies the body of Christ.

If your worship leader, pastor, or preacher ever directed the church to take a praise break, then this praise break is likely a response to some attribute of God or to the word of God being preached. A praise break is classified as a spontaneous sound. A praise break may even inspire others to engage in a praise break, but the reasoning behind the individual praise breaks is completely independent of one another because a praise break is like speaking in tongues between you and God. It is not meant for anyone else to understand. More on prophetic sound and its ability to edify the body of Christ will be elaborated upon in the second principle.

**Principle 2:** **Spontaneous sound** is a movement that is inspired by a message but is not a manifestation of the message that inspired it; **prophetic sound**

contains a message (revelation, knowledge, prophecy, or word of instruction) that manifests itself as a movement.

The message is the movement, and the movement is the message. Like the first principle, spontaneous sound is inspired by a message.

**Principle 3: Spontaneous sound** does not require interpretation or intelligibility; **prophetic sound** is eligible for interpretation or intelligibility.

Think about it; we do not need intellect to praise God. Even in Jesus's encounter with the woman at the well, He tells her that Samaritans worship what they do not know, while the Jews worship what they do know (John 4:22). There is a clear distinction that a person can worship God without having any intellectual basis. However, do not get confused. While we are drawing the line between spontaneous and prophetic sound, is not an argument to prove that one sound is better than the other. I will discuss that issue at another time.

Even though we do not require intellect to praise God, we are encouraged to pursue gifts, which include the ability to prophesy or function prophetically. When you begin to prophesy or worship prophetically, then your song, dance, motion, and artwork are all automatically subject to interpretation and intelligibility.

**Principle 4:** **Spontaneous sound** surpasses our understanding, while **prophetic sound** requires the ability to understand.

Like intellect, you do not need understanding to praise God, requiring extraordinarily little thought, discipline, and responsibility, thus, making it spontaneous. The prophetic sound has a higher degree of responsibility. If you are releasing a prophetic sound, that means you must have an idea of how your gift works and functions when it is actually in operation. Even when an individual prophesies, the interpretation and understanding may not be with the one who prophesies, but someone in the vicinity may be able to interpret the message embedded in an instrumental solo, a dance motif, or artwork. Understanding must be a requisite because a prophecy that is misunderstood might as well be dead. We know that God's word does not fall to the ground as dead, but we do know that if a person does not pursue to understand the promises presented to them through prophecy, then the prophetic word or sound is at risk of not manifesting or exhibiting a delayed manifestation within the life of the individual whom the message was for.

**Principle 5:** **Spontaneous sound** is already perfect; **prophetic sound** requires training and perfecting.

The word informs us that everything that has breath has the capacity to praise the Lord. We are even instructed to make a joyful noise unto the Lord. This implies that spontaneous sound is already perfect as creation participates in this praise. Spontaneous sound does not require the same level of discipline and training, as it is classified as a noise. One can discipline themselves to release a spontaneous sound unto the Lord, but the sound itself requires no training whatsoever. For example, I used to carry a worship timer that would buzz every seven minutes and twenty-seven seconds. Each time the buzzer went off, I would release a spontaneous praise to the Lord if it did not cause a distraction. (I would often wear this worship timer while at work). However, again, spontaneous sound does not carry with it the same responsibilities as a prophetic sound. Releasing a prophetic sound requires training and perfecting. The gift to release a prophetic sound is perfect, but the skill, wisdom, and prudence required to release it is not perfect. It requires a great deal of discipline to effectively use the gift of prophecy.

If you really want to separate the two types of sound, spontaneous sound does not require a direct translation of what you hear in the spirit. It is a response to what you hear in the spirit, and this spontaneous praise is meant to create the momentum for your personal breakthrough and no one else's. Prophetic sound is about taking what you hear in the heavenly realms and doing whatever it takes to release that word in this realm. You have to search for the proper language and movement in order to accurately express something that is spiritual. The prophetic sound creates opportunities of breakthrough for others because it is a tool for edification.

## 08 – Sound Amplification

Amplification means "to expand on something, such as a statement, by the use of detail or illustration or by closer analysis" (Merriam-Webster Dictionary). Spontaneous sound is good, but it only amplifies and magnifies God because spontaneous sound is a response to a message. On the other hand, prophetic sound is able to amplify and magnify the message that is coming from the heart of God.

Even in music, music sounds louder when the melodies are played in tune and unison. When you break into harmony, the melody sounds fuller and richer. However, if you create too many moving parts, you eventually will take a distinguishable sound and drown it in noise. The collective sound is not amplified.

In dance and movement-based ministries, the sound of dance is louder if multiple dancers perform the same choreography and use the same instruments. This is another reason why spontaneous sound or dance does not amplify a message. They only amplify what is specifically happening as a result of communion with God within that specific individual. The sound and movement from everyone are on completely different frequencies and rhythms. Just as there are diversities of tongues, there are diversities of rhythms and movements, each producing its own language. Pure spontaneous dance unto the Lord simply produces a spontaneous noise, which is not a bad thing.

57

## Which is Better?  Spontaneous or Prophetic Sound

One of the moral issues that must be addressed concerning the use of prophetic and spontaneous worship is that some audiences think that one is better than the other.  Some have even considered that certain church's music ministries are better because they do more prophetic or spontaneous worship than others.  Just as Paul warns the Corinthian church about being enamored with the gifts, the same goes for worship arts.  We can spontaneously move without love.  This is what happens when we try to turn praise breaks into entertainment or religious routine.  We can prophetically move without love because some people have perfected their praise (or worship) in such a way that it becomes a performance and operates on its own.

Therefore, both spontaneous and prophetic sounds can become a noise that does not communicate anything valuable into the atmosphere.  If an individual tries to exalt spontaneous or prophetic worship over different forms of worship, then the individual moves into the sin of pride and steps out of operating in love.  If you have ever envied or coveted another worshipper's gifts, abilities, demonstrations, musicianship, pageantry, dance, or vocal ability, then you have risked becoming a sound that produces meaningless noise.  As a worship artist, you must press in to being enamored by God and not by gifts.

## Amplification by Fire

Here is the reason why neither spontaneous worship nor prophetic worship is better than one another. God can choose to amplify the sound by baptizing the sound or movement in fire. When God really wants a specific message to be heard, regardless of it being spontaneous or prophetic, He will baptize it in fire for it to catch someone's attention. Consider the burning bush in the desert during Moses's lifetime as a shepherd. The fact that the bush was not consumed was what drew Moses to it. When he arrived, he received a message from the Lord.

Now, this next example may be more convincing. Consider the day of Pentecost in Acts 2. The wind blew through the believers, tongues of fire rested upon each of them, and being filled with the Holy Spirit, they spoke in other tongues as the Spirit enabled. They were each declaring the wonders of God in their own personal conversations with the Lord. However, because the Lord had sent fire upon them, their individual conversations with God could be heard, interpreted, and understood by the Jews visiting from other nations. Even though this event appeared to be a spontaneous moment of worship, God still allowed it to be heard.

So, what does all of this mean? Whether you are worshipping spontaneously or prophetically, if God sends fire on your worship, whatever message is in the conversation of that worship will be amplified by God for specific people groups to supernaturally see and understand. Ultimately, the fire speaks to the people whom you are destined to deliver from bondage. He gives you a language and a message that can only be heard by people of specific ethnicities, cultural backgrounds, hurts, pains, trials, victories, profession, etc. If a person can identify with your personal experience, God can light fire to it and use it to stir up a holy conversation to another individual from your place of worship.

## 09 – Additional Challenges of Spontaneous and Prophetic Sound

Dealing with Imposters in Worship Arts

> Nevertheless, I have this against you: You tolerate that woman Jezebel, who calls herself a prophet. By her teaching, she misleads my servants into sexual immorality and the eating of food sacrificed to idols. I have given her time to repent of her immorality, but she is unwilling. (Revelation 2:20-21, NIV)

Too many people call themselves something that they are not, and that is a spirit of Jezebel. When you try to exalt yourself into a title or position that you do not have the authority to operate in, you run the risk of misleading people. It also includes using your operation in certain gifts as evidence of your authority to hold a position or title. This is why artists are not respected in the church; too many call themselves prophetic but are just spontaneous worshippers.

I am a spontaneous musician. It is quite easy to do this. I did study some jazz when I was in school, and improvisation can be taught. However, when I play prophetically, I ask God, "what would you like for me to play?" I often ask this question before I step into the musician's pit or even during worship. Even if I have already rehearsed a song

61

thousands of times with a band, I will still ask God, "Is there anything you want me to play differently today?" What makes this prophetic is that I am asking God for a message to release in my music from His eternal repertoire of music.

Whenever there are praise breaks, I enjoy giving God spontaneous praise; however, I am not a prophetic dancer, nor will I ever claim that my dance is prophetic. One summer, I did a series of livestreams on Facebook. I would close the livestream by waving swing flags. People would try to call me a flagger, but I would have to correct them and say that I am a worshipper who is using flags as an instrument to express my worship. I simply do not have enough skill to be a flagger. I cannot prophesy with flags as some people are skilled to do. However, I do know that I am anointed to release prophetic sounds because an anointed prophetess activated that gift in me.

Meanwhile, you have some people who boastfully call themselves the spontaneous sect when there is nothing to boast about. People know this, but they are too uneducated to put a language and understanding to identifying these people other than to call them hypocrites. Whether you are a musician, singer, dancer, mime, etc., spontaneous worship and prophetic worship are not the same. Therefore, you may need to repent and apologize to some church leaders and people you minister with after this teaching.

We do not even have respect for the people we minister with and the people we minister to. We lie to our fellow ministers and lie about who we are without even saying anything. This type of behavior can turn us worship artists into hypocrites. God does not like pride and arrogance. So, let God deal with it.

The Sound of Worship Being Silenced

**What do I do if I've been operating in the prophetic, but ministry team members are shutting me out?** Then you must allow God to handle the situation. Ask Him if and how He wants to make room for your prophetic gift in the body of Christ. Never do anything out of order in the church.

While playing during a typical church service with the band, and a fellow musician attempted to tell me to stop playing. I was so offended; I was ready to chop off the musician's head with my tongue. Instead of doing that, I told the Lord that I know I could spiritually decapitate him, but I refuse to engage him in conversation because if I do, I will cut his head off with my tongue. Whether or not he knew of the prophetic, I was angry that he tried to tell me what to do in the middle of the service, especially since he was not the lead music director, worship leader, or pastor. None of the leaders had told me or signaled me to stop playing. In order to avoid the temptation of using my tongue as a weapon of evil, I excused myself from the musician's pit.

The musician knew that I was mad and had messaged me because he said he wanted to talk about what happened.  Again, to avoid temptation, I messaged him back.  I told him that I refuse to discuss the matter amongst the two of us because I already know exactly how this conversation will end.  We can proceed to have this discussion in the presence of a third party, who is of higher authority than the both of us.  I knew this fellow musician to be quite adamant and passionate in his argumentation skills.  Because of my personality, I have two approaches for people like this.  Either I just silently sit through the argument and allow the individual to win, or I will intellectually demolish the individual to the point that it could strain our relationship.  I have little patience for people who try to speak on things that they are ignorant about, and this situation was one of those moments of low patience.  Anyway, after I had sent the message to this musician, I heard nothing back.

Within 48 hours, the musician called me and said he took personal initiation to investigate the issue by talking to our pastor.  He let me know that he was corrected on the matter, and he apologized for stepping into my territory as a musician.  His apology meant a lot because our relationship was kept intact, and I could continue to trust him as a fellow musician who was maturing in leadership skills.  In the end, if someone disrespects your prophetic ministry, let this testimony serve as an example of how God can handle it if you hand it over to Him.  I am not the type of musician who openly prophesies a lot with my instrument, but the Lord continued to make room as He saw fit. Regardless, I did not like the idea of my gift being controlled by someone who did not understand it at the time. Thankfully, God allowed someone of higher authority to take care of it on my behalf without me having to be in the meeting. At the end of the day, whether you consider yourself a spontaneous or prophetic worshipper, do not use your knowledge of this to exert authority over anyone else and step out of order in your local church or ministry.

## Closing Prayer

Father, I praise and thank You for being the One who created all things. I thank You for creating worship before the foundations of the earth and creating a plan for us to be divine participants in worshipping You with all our heart, mind, soul, and strength through the sacrifice of Your Son, Jesus. I thank You for giving us Your Spirit so that we can understand what it means to worship You in Spirit and in truth to enable us to partner with You in subduing the earth.

Father, I pray that You would continue to give revelatory knowledge of Jesus Christ to myself and all those who will follow these teachings in dance musicality. I pray that everyone who follows these teachings will humbly embrace these truths so that they may experience greater measures of the power associated with developing a worshipful lifestyle, whether it is in music, dance, mime, ministry, business, or career work. May we all be captivated by Christ so that our sound may be clear and uncontaminated, and all creation can rejoice with us as we worship. May we cast down any thought and imagination that exalts itself against the knowledge of You so that we can become properly constructed temples for your Holy Spirit. May we develop a cloud consciousness that will help us turn from the temptations of sin and embrace the weight of Your glory, that we can endure in our faith toward You.

We thank and praise You for allowing us to carry the sound of heaven in us so that we might go forth and liberate all creation through the power of the gospel of Jesus Christ! It is in the name of Jesus that we pray; amen!

## About the Author

**EUAL PHILLIPS** is a native of Houma, Louisiana and currently resides in Philadelphia, Pennsylvania, working as a high school science educator. As he was earning his master's degree in biomedical engineering at the University of Pennsylvania, Eual served as a deacon, musician, and intercessor within his local church and developed a passion for explaining the dynamics of worship arts through the application of Christian and scientific principles. Additionally, Eual is an independent recording artist and serves as a board member of Christ Center for Dance and the Arts.

For more information regarding Eual Phillips and his multi-faceted ministry and the latest teachings on musicality and worship arts, visit www.eualphillips.com.

For more information about taking on-demand courses or becoming a student of Christ Center for Dance and the Arts – School of Ministry, visit www.christcenterfordance.org.

## Additional Books by the Author

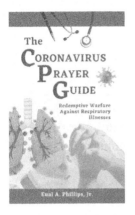

The Coronavirus Prayer Guide:  Redemptive Warfare
Against Respiratory Illnesses

Spiritual Standards of Teaching:  a 10-Day
Devotional for Educators

71

# Bibliography

*Dolmetsch Online Music Dictionary.* 2015a. Articulation. http://www. dolmetsch.com/defst1.htm (accessed January 9, 2021).

———. 2015b. Canon. http://www.dolmetsch.com/defst1.htm (accessed January 9, 2021).

———. 2015c. Rhythmic variation. http://www.dolmetsch.com/ defst1.htm (accessed January 9, 2021).

Grant, L., 2017. Enhancing Musicality in Ballet Technique Classes. *Dance Education in Practice*, *3*(3), pp.20-26.

Kuhn, L. 1999. Beat. In *Baker's student encyclopedia of music.* Vol. 1, A-G, ed. L. Kuhn, 99. New York: Schirmer Reference.

Latham, A. 2002. Tempo. In *The Oxford companion to music,* ed. A. Latham. New York: Oxford University Press.

Randel, D. 1986. Meter. In *The new Harvard dictionary of music,* ed. D. Randel, 489. Cambridge, MA: Belknap.

Made in the USA
Monee, IL
26 August 2023